FLOWER

HENRY LLOYD was born a ___
Etonhurst and Canford School. ___
and then went to Cuddesdon ___ ___. A curacy at
Hendon St Mary's was followed by the outbreak of World War II, when
he joined the Royal Navy and served as chaplain in the aircraft carrier
H.M.S. *Illustrious*. He was awarded the D.S.O. by King George VI
in1941. He later joined the famous battle cruiser H.M.S. *Renown*. In
1950 he was appointed Dean of the cathedral in Gibraltar and in 1959 was
awarded the O.B.E.. In 1960 he was called to Cornwall to become the first
Dean of Truro, where his work for the cathedral was acknowledged with
the distinction of Honoured Citizen.

From an early age he kept a line book of thoughts and quotations,
which gave him tremendous encouragement over the years and especially in coming to terms with his unexpected blindness during his
retirement. It is his wish that this book may shine for others with the
same message of hope. Henry Lloyd now lives with his wife in Dorset.
Their only daughter is now married and has recently given birth to their
first grandchild, who brings them great joy.

FELICITY REDMAN was born in England, and spent the early years
of her childhood in Gibraltar where her father was Governor. Encour-
aged to draw from the moment she was old enough to hold a pencil, and
influenced by the artistic talents of mother and grandmother, she has
continued to develop her own distinctive style. Her love of adventure
has led her to over 37 countries, including voyaging across oceans in
small sailing yachts, climbing volcanoes and mountains, filming whales
in the Indian Ocean and exploring ancient temples deep in the tropical
jungle. Each expedition results in a series of miniature illustrations, full
of hidden details which are so often unnoticed by people in "too much
of a hurry." She works out in the open whenever possible and draws
much inspiration from being close to nature. Her work and card
collections are to be found in various parts of the world. When not
travelling she lives in Dorset.

"... so pass the waves ..." (Prayer at Baptism, p.11)

FLOWERS
OF THE FIELD

An Anthology of Hope

Compiled by
HENRY LLOYD

With illustrations by
FELICITY REDMAN

BURNS & OATES

First published 1996

BURNS & OATES,
Wellwood, North Farm Road,
Tunbridge Wells, Kent TN2 3DR

Compilation and nos. 46, 50, 56, 82 Copyright © 1996 by Henry M. Lloyd
Illustrations Copyright © 1996 by Felicity Redman

ISBN 0 86012 264 6

COMPILER'S ACKNOWLEDGEMENTS
I am most grateful to Miss Felicity Redman for undertaking the illustrations for this anthology and to Mrs Beauclerk for her unfailing help and advice.

Extracts from *Collected Poems 1909–1962* and *The Rock* by T. S. Eliot are reprinted by permission of Faber & Faber Ltd; from *Recreation of an Historian* by G. M. Trevelyan by permission of the Longman Group; from *Civilization* by Kenneth Clark by permission of John Murray (Publishers) Ltd; from *Period of my Life* by F. R. Barry by permission of Hodder & Stoughton. The compiler has made every effort to trace copyright holders: any not here acknowledged are invited to contact the publishers.

Typeset by Search Press Limited
Printed in Great Britain by BPC Wheatons Ltd, Exeter

FOREWORD

Early in 1940, HMS Illustrious, the first of a new class of aircraft carrier, was commissioned at Barrow-in-Furness under the command of Denis Boyd (later to become Admiral Sir Denis Boyd).

Nearly a year later she was severely damaged by German dive bombers in the Central Mediterranean, and during the next fourteen days endured further heavy attacks and damage in Malta while temporary repairs were effected. For his work with the wounded and with the Ship's Company generally during that peiod, Henry Lloyd was awarded the D.S.O..

It was at this time and during subsequent months that my own faith started to grow and take shape; and it is for this reason only that a complete nonentity is very happy to attempt this Foreword; for Henry Lloyd was one of three triggers in a change to my life which culminated in my own ordination twenty years later.

Exactly what Henry said or did to put me on a right road to prayer I cannot remember; but these "Flowers" strike a chord that takes me back nearly 55 years, while yet holding, for me, an equally telling relevance for today.

In short, an anthology of encouragement and hope.

I.F.W.

... and He led me towards the hills and the breaking of the day

1

I said to the man who stood at the gate of the year, "Give me a light that I may tread safely into the unknown." And he replied, "Go out into the darkness and put your hand into the hand of God. That shall be to you better than light, and safer than any known way." So I went forth, and finding the hand of God trod gladly into the night, and He led me towards the hills and the breaking of the day.

LOUISE HASKINS
Quoted by King George VI
on Christmas Day 1939

2

It is an ironic fact that in this nuclear age, when the horizon of human knowledge and human experience has passed far beyond any that any age has ever known, that we turn back at this time to the older source of wisdom and strength, to the words of the Prophets and Saints, who tell us that

> *FAITH* is more powerful than doubt,
> *HOPE* is more powerful than despair,
>> And that only through the love that is
>> sometimes called
> *CHARITY* can we conquer those forces within ourselves
>> and throughout the world, that threaten the very
>> existence of humanity.

JOHN F. KENNEDY

3

It is lack of confidence, more than anything else, that kills a civilization. We can destroy ourselves by cynicism and disillusion, just as effectively as by bombs.

KENNETH CLARK: *Civilization*

4

And yet show I unto you a more excellent way. Though I speak with the tongues of men and of angels, and have not charity, I am become as sounding brass or a tinkling cymbal.

1 Corinthians 12:31; 13:1

5

As a whole
We are a generation of men
So estranged from the inner
    world
That many are arguing
That it does not exist,
And that even if it does exist
It does not matter.
For without the inner
The outer loses its meaning
And without the outer
The inner loses its substance.

Anon.

6

Endless invention, endless experiment
Brings knowledge of motion, but not of stillness;
Knowledge of speech, but not of silence;
Knowledge of words, and ignorance of the Word.
Where is the Life we have lost in living?
Where is the wisdom we have lost in knowledge?
Where is the knowledge we have lost in information?

T. S. ELIOT: Choruses of *The Rock*

7

The settled happiness and security which we all desire is withheld from us by the very nature of the world, but joy and merriment are to be found all along the way. We are never safe, we may suffer much, but we have plenty of fun. Our heavenly Father refreshes us on the journey with many good friends.

Based on C. S. LEWIS

8

Merriment is the birthright of the young. But we can all keep it in our hearts as life goes on, if we hold fast by the Spirit that refuses to admit defeat, by the faith that never falters, by the hope that cannot be quenched.

KING GEORGE VI
BBC Radio Broadcast, 15 August 1945

9

So that being steadfast in faith, joyful through hope and rooted in charity, may we in our time so pass the waves of this troublesome world, and finally come to the land of everlasting life.

Prayer at Baptism

10

A mighty spiritual force streams forth from Jesus—in Him is the supreme spiritual and religious authority.

The conviction of ALBERT SCHWEITZER

11

This seems a cheerful world, Donatus, when I view it from this fair garden, under the shade of these vines. But, if I climbed some great mountain and looked out over the wide lands, you know very well what I would see: brigands on the high roads, pirates on the seas, in the amphitheatres men murdered to please the applauding crowds, under many roofs misery and selfishness. It is really a bad world, Donatus, an incredibly bad world. But in the midst of it I have found a quiet and holy people. They have discovered a joy which is a thousand times better than any pleasure of this sinful life. They are despised and persecuted, but they care not. They have overcome the world. These people, Donatus, are the Christians ... and I am one of them.

ST CYPRIAN writing to Donatus in the third century:
Quoted by Dr. Coggan
at his enthronement at Canterbury

12

And this is the victory that overcometh the world, our faith.

1 John 5:4

13

That God does not exist, I cannot deny. That my whole being cries out for God, I cannot forget.

JEAN-PAUL SARTRE

14

God grant me the courage to change the things I can change, the serenity to accept those I cannot change, and the wisdom to know the difference.

Anon.

15

The glory of life
Is to love, not to be loved.
To serve, not to be served.
To be a strong hand in the dark
To another in time of need,
To be a cup of strength to any soul
In a crisis of weakness.
This is to know the glory of life.

Anon.

A cup of strength

16

Let nothing disturb thee
Let nothing dismay thee
All things pass
God never changes.
He who has God
Finds he lacks nothing,
God alone suffices. Amen.

ST TERESA OF AVILA

17

Tablet above the west door of Staunton Harold Church in Leicestershire:

> In the yeare 1653—when all things sacred were throughout ye nation either demolisht or profaned—Sir Robert Shirley, Baronet, founded this church; whose singular praise it is, to have done the best things in ye worst times and hoped them in the most calamitous. The righteous shall be had in everlasting remembrance.

This loyalty to God and King was to cost Sir Robert his life. Cromwell sent him to the Tower to face death, aged twenty-seven.

18

No coward soul is mine,
No trembler in the world's storm-troubled sphere:
I see Heaven's glories shine,
And faith shines equal, arming me from fear,
Though earth and man were gone
And sons and universes ceased to be
And Thou were left alone
Every existence would exist in Thee.

Last poem of EMILY BRONTË

19

*Helen Keller, thanks to the skill and patience, prayer and faith of her
friend and mentor, Anne Sullivan, out of a childhood of deafness,
blindness and dumbness, became one of the most brilliant and
distinguished, loved and admired women of her time. She wrote:*

It is no good saying, "Why has this happened to me?"; but as it has
happened, what are we going to do about it? When such things
happen, we should take the initiative, look into ourselves fear-
lessly, search out new ideas of what to do and how to develop our
will power. Then God will give us enough light and love for all
our needs.

HELEN KELLER

20

There shall always be the Church and the world
And the heart of man
Shivering and fluttering between them,
Choosing and chosen
Valiant, ignoble, dark and full of light
Swinging between Hell Gate and Heaven Gate,
And the Gates of Hell shall not prevail
Darkness now, then Light ... Light

T. S. ELIOT: Choruses of *The Rock*

21

Inscription on a stone in a
Cotswold garden:

       Hours fly
       Flowers die
       New days
       New ways
       Pass by
       Love stays

... a sudden shaft of sunlight ...

22

The Kingdoms of the earth go by
In purple and in gold
They rise, they triumph and they die
And all their tale is told.

One Kingdom only is divine
One Empire triumphs still
Its King a Servant, and its sign
A cross upon a hill.

Anon.

23

Whilst walking up Ludgate Hill on the way to St Paul's for Ordination, a sudden shaft of sunlight pierced the grey skies illuminating the cross at the top of the dome, proclaiming its eternal message:

Shine through the gloom
and point me to the skies:
Heaven's morning breaks,
and earth's vain shadows flee;
In life, in death, O Lord, abide with me

H. F. LYTE: "Abide with Me"

24

Little did we know, at the beginning of this century, of the terrible events that would engulf the world ... the supreme sacrifice:

> In Flanders' fields the poppies grow
> Between the crosses row on row
> That mark our place: and in the sky
> The larks still bravely singing fly
> Scarce heard amid the guns below.
> We are the dead—short days ago
> We lived, felt dawn, saw sunset glow
> Loved, and were loved, and now we lie
> In Flanders' Fields.

JOHN McCRAE: *"In Flanders' Fields"*

25

This renowned epitaph is a free translation from the address by Leonidas to the Spartans after the battle of Thermopylae:

> When you go home
> Tell them of us and say
> For your tomorrow
> We gave our to-day.

26

The Saviour said: "In the world ye shall have tribulation; but be of good cheer; for I have overcome the world."

John 16:33

27

Put thou thy trust in God
In duty's path go on
Walk in His strength with faith and hope
So shall thy work be done.

JOHN WESLEY: Hymn

28

He said not thou shalt not be tempested
Thou shalt not be travailed
Thou shalt not be afflicted
But he said thou shalt not be overcome.

Dame JULIAN OF NORWICH

29

There in that other world, what waits for me?
What shall I find after that other birth?
No stormy, tossing, foaming, smiling sea—but a new earth.

No sun to mark the changing of the days
No soft falling of the alternate night
No moon, no stars, no light upon my way—only the Light.

No grey cathedral, wide and wondrous fair
That I may tread where all my fathers trod
Nay, nay my soul, no House of God is there—only God.

MARY COLERIDGE

30

For everything in this world comes to an end, blows itself out like
a summer storm, save only the love of God.

Spanish proverb

31

Hope, like a gleaming taper's light
Adorns and cheers our way—
And still as darker grows the night
Emits a brighter ray.

OLIVER GOLDSMITH

32

Best trust the happy moments. What they gave
Makes man less fearful of the certain grave
And gives his work compassion and new eyes
The days that make us happy make us wise.

JOHN MASEFIELD: *Biography*

33

Bright is the ring of words
When the right man rings them,
Fair the fall of songs
When the singer sings them.
Still they are carolled and said—
On wings they are carried—
After the singer is dead
And the maker buried.

R. L. STEVENSON: *Songs of Farewell*

... a myriad scattered stars ...

34

In the castle of my soul there is a little postern gate
Where, when I enter, I am in the presence of God.
In a moment, in the turning of a thought,
I am where God is.
When I meet God there, all life gains a new meaning,
Small things become great, and great things small.
Lowly and despised things are shot through,
My troubles seem but pebbles on the road, with glory.
My joys seem like the everlasting hills,
All my fever is gone in the great peace of God
And I pass through the door from time into Eternity.

WALTER RAUSCHENBUSCH

35

The healing of the world is in its nameless saints. Each separate
star seems nothing, but a myriad scattered stars break up the
night and make it beautiful.

BAYARD TAYLOR

36

I walked a mile with Pleasure,
She chatted all the way,
But left me none the wiser
For all she had to say.
I walked a mile with Sorrow
And ne'er a word said she;
But, Oh, the things I learned from her
When sorrow walked with me.

ROBERT B. HAMILTON: "Along the Road"

37

Because the way was steep and long
And through a strange and lonely land
God placed upon my lips a song
And put a lantern in my hand.

JOYCE KILMER

38

We are often completely blind to the emotional feelings and the needs of others, even as they are completely blind to ours, and it is possible for people to live and work in close proximity to others and know nothing of their loneliness and the crisis which they are undergoing.

F. J. BRACELAND

39

Thanks to the human heart by which we live
Thanks to its tenderness—its joys and fears,
To me the meanest flower that blows can give
Thoughts that do often lie, too deep for tears.

WILLIAM WORDSWORTH:
"Ode on Intimations of Immortality"

... the meanest flower that blows
can give
Thoughts that do often lie, too
deep for tears.

The poppy saith amid the corn

40

Flowers preach to us if we will hear,
The rose saith in the dewy morn;
I am most fair;
Yet all my loveliness is born
Upon a thorn.
The poppy saith amid the corn;
Let but my scarlet head appear
And I am held in scorn.
Yet juice of subtle virtue lies
Within my cup of curious dyes.
The lilies say: behold how we
Preach without words ... of purity.
The violets whisper from the shade
Which their own leaves have made;
Men scent our fragrance on the air
Yet take no heed
Of humble lessons we would read.
But not alone the fairest flowers:
The merest grass
Along the roadside where we pass,
Lichen and moss and sturdy weed,
Tell of His love who sends the dew,
The rain and sunshine too
To nourish one small seed.

CHRISTINA ROSSETTI

Flower in the crannied wall ...

41

Flower in the crannied wall,
I pluck you out of the crannies,
I hold you here, root and all, in my hand,
Little flower—but if I could understand
What you are, root and all, and all in all,
I should know what God and man is.

ALFRED, LORD TENNYSON:
"Flower in the crannied wall"

Amid the delicate and
bladed wheat
That springs triumphant in
the furrowed sod

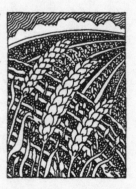

42

I come, saith the Lord, in the little things
Not borne on morning wings
Of majesty; but I have set my feet
Amid the delicate and bladed wheat
That springs triumphant in the furrowed sod.
There I dwell in weakness and in power
Not broken or divided saith our God.

EVELYN UNDERHILL

43

The corn that makes the holy Bread
By which the soul of man is fed,
The holy Bread the food unpriced
Thy everlasting mercy Christ.

JOHN MASEFIELD

44

God was the Word and spake it
He took the Bread and brake it
And what that Word doth make it
I do believe and take it.

QUEEN ELIZABETH I

45

There is no door that enough love will not open
No gulf that enough love will not bridge
No wall that enough love will not throw down
No sin that enough love will not redeem.

The Cloud of Unknowing

46

Heaven defend us from a closed mind or from a mind so open there is nothing in it.

H. M. Ll.

47

Laugh and the world laughs with you;
Weep, and you weep alone,
For the sad old earth must borrow its mirth,
But has trouble enough of its own.

ELLA WHEELER WILCOX: "Solitude"

48

He that is down, needs fear no fall,
He that is low, no pride;
He that is humble, ever shall
Have God to be his guide.
I am content with what I have
Little be it or much;
And Lord contentment still I crave
Because Thou savest such.

JOHN BUNYAN:
"Song of the Shepherd Boy"

... having expected to find it barren I was astonished to see it covered with beautiful wild narcissi ...

49

On a huge hill
Cragged and steep, truth stands,
And he that will reach her,
About, and about must go.

JOHN DONNE

50

I remember, during my first Christmas in Gibraltar, climbing to
the summit of The Rock, and having expected to find it barren I
was astonished to see it covered with beautiful wild narcissi—like
the flowers of the field, speaking the truth that endureth for ever.

H. M. Ll.

51

It fortifies my soul to know
That though I perish truth is so
That howso'er I stray and range
I steadier step when I recall
That if I slip—Thou dost not fall.

ARTHUR HUGH CLOUGH:
Quoted by William Temple *in his last address
to Ordinands*

52

Words can be very powerful
They can make us friends or enemies
They can make war or peace
They can save life or destroy it.

Anon.

53

Man's unhappiness, as I construe, comes of his greatness; it is
because there is an Infinite in him, which with all his cunning he
cannot quite bury under the Finite.

THOMAS CARLYLE

54

They [men] constantly try to escape
From the darkness outside and within
By dreaming of systems so perfect
     that no one will need to be good.
But the man that is will shadow
The man that pretends to be.

T.S. ELIOT: Choruses of *The Rock*

55

Make us worthy Lord to serve our fellow men throughout the
world who live and die in poverty and hunger. Give them
through our hands this day our daily bread, and by our understanding love, give peace and joy.

MOTHER TERESA'S prayer

56

Worship is not an escape from reality, on the contrary, it is an
entering into the heart and soul of our existence.

H. M. Ll.

57

All shall be well,
and all shall be well
and all manner of things shall be well.

These words of Dame JULIAN's, greatly loved by the mother of Queen Elizabeth II, spring from a deeply rooted faith in the goodness of God.

58

Faith has had many an hour of doubt and darkness, but the darkness has not overcome it. What supports the individual pilgrim is the faith and experience of the Church. The foundation of that Faith is not in ideas which must change with the changing movements of secular thought, but in the historical and living Christ, the same yesterday, today, and for ever. Other foundation can no man lay.

F. R. BARRY: *Period of my Life*

59

Dear God, be good to me, my boat is so small
and the sea is so wide.

A fisherman's prayer

60

Whither shall I go from thy spirit?
Or whither shall I flee from thy presence?
If I climb up into Heaven—thou art there;
If I go down to hell, thou art there also;
If I take the wings of the morning, and remain
In the uttermost parts of the sea;
Even there also shall thy hand lead me,
And thy right hand shall hold me.

Psalm 139

Here in this little bay ...

61

Here in this little bay
Full of tumultuous life and great repose
Where twice a day
The purposeless, glad ocean comes and goes,
Under high cliffs and far from the huge town
I sit me down.
For want of me the world's course will not fail
When all its work is done, the lie shall rot.
The truth is great and shall prevail,
When none cares whether it prevail or not.

COVENTRY PATMORE

62

John Donne gave Isaak Walton one of the signet rings he devised for his friends—the figure of Christ on the cross depicted as an anchor (1615):

The Cross, my seal in Baptism, spread below
Doth by that form into an anchor grow.
Crosses grow anchors, bear as thou shouldst do
Thy cross, and that cross grows an anchor too.
But He that makes our crosses anchors thus
Is Christ, who there is crucified for us.

JOHN DONNE

41

63

And the stately ships go on
To their haven under the hill
But O for the touch of a   .
    vanished hand
And the sound of a voice that is
    still.

Break, break, break
At the foot of the crags, O sea!
But the tender grace of a day
    that is dead
Will never come back to me.

ALFRED, LORD TENNYSON:
"Break, break, break," *In Memoriam V*

64

Just as a good mariner, when he draws near to the harbour, lets down his sails and enters it gently, with slight headway on, so ought we to let down the sails of our worldly pursuits and turn to God with all our understanding and all our heart, so that we may come to Him with all composure and with all peace.

DANTE

65

Sunset and evening star,
And one clear call for me!
And may there be no moaning at the bar,
When I put out to sea.
But such a tide as moving seems asleep,
Too full for sound and foam,
When that which drew from out the boundless deep,
Turns again home.

Twilight and evening bell,
And after that the dark!
And may there be no sadness of farewell,
When I embark;
For tho' from out our bourne of Time and Place,
The flood may bear me far,
I hope to see my Pilot face to face,
When I have crost the bar.

ALFRED, LORD TENNYSON:
"Crossing the Bar"

66

The Parson addresses Saul, the rebellious young man, in John Masefield's poem "The Everlasting Mercy":

To get the whole world out of bed
And washed and dressed and warmed and fed
To work and back to bed again
Believe me, Saul, costs worlds of pain.
Then, as to whether true or sham
The Book of Christ whose priest I am
The Bible is a lie, say you
Where do you stand, suppose it true?

JOHN MASEFIELD

67

Whether we be young or old,
Our destiny, our being's heart and home,
Is with infinitude, and only there.

WILLIAM WORDSWORTH: *The Prelude, Book VI*

68

Disapprove—if you must—go on
disapproving, but never let your
disapproval enter into your soul.

Anon.

69

I fled Him, down the nights and down the days;
I fled Him, down the arches of the years;
I fled Him, down the labyrinthine ways
Of my own mind; and in the midst of tears
I hid from Him, and under running laughter.

But with unhurrying chase,
And unperturb'd pace,
Deliberate speed, majestic instancy,
They beat—and a Voice beat
More instant than the Feet—
"All things betray thee, who betrayest Me."

FRANCIS THOMPSON: *The Hound of Heaven*

70

And not till the loom is silent
And the shuttles cease to fly
Will God unfold the canvas
And explain the reason why.
The dark threads are as useful
In the Weaver's skilful hand,
As the threads of gold and silver
In the pattern He has planned.

Anon.

71

They are all gone into the world of light
And I alone sit lingering here.
Their very memory is fair and bright
And my sad thoughts doth clear.

HENRY VAUGHAN

72

It is absurd to suppose that the Christian virtues which cement a
caring community, the Christian view of death which transforms
life, the Christian ethics without which law and order crumble,
can survive without the belief which formed them.

Anon.

73

The world turns and the world changes,
But one thing does not change.
In all of my years, one thing does not change.
However you disguise it, this thing does not change:
The perpetual struggle of Good and Evil.

T. S. ELIOT: Choruses of *The Rock*

74

Things fall apart, the centre cannot hold;
Mere anarchy is loosed upon the world.
The blood-dimmed tide is loosed, and everywhere
The ceremony of innocence is drowned.
The best lack all conviction, while the worst
Are full of passionate intensity.

W. B. YEATS: "The Second Coming"

75

What is vital to recover are the moral and spiritual foundations upon which the lives of both the individual and our civilization depend. To bring home to the average man that religion is not a pious fiction which has nothing to do with the actual facts of life, but that it is concerned with realities, that it is, in fact, the pathway to reality and the law of life.

CHRISTOPHER DAWSON

76

Materialism offers us a hopeless end.
Christianity offers us endless hope.

Anon.

77

There are times when we can never meet the future with sufficient
elasticity of mind, especially if we are locked in the contemporary
systems of thought. We can do worse than to remember a
principle which both gives us a firm rock and leaves us the
maximum elasticity for our minds: the principle "Hold to Christ
and for the rest be totally uncommitted."

HERBERT BUTTERFIELD

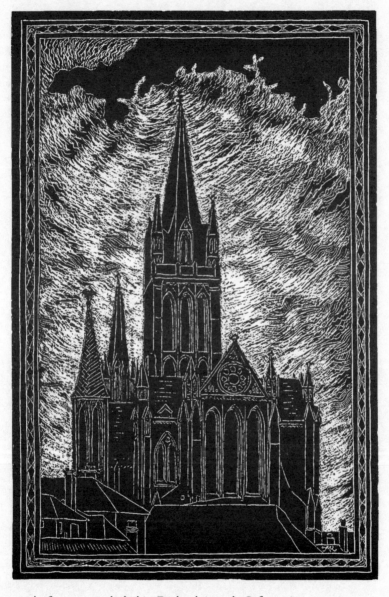

... the first great cathedral in England since the Reformation

78

Discouraged in the work of life
Disheartened by its load
Shamed by its foulness and its fears,
I sink beside the road:
But only let me think of Thee
And then new hope springs up in me.

H. W. LONGFELLOW

79

*At the end of a long and rather disappointing day's fundraising in the
City, for the building of Truro Cathedral, Bishop Benson made his
way wearily to Evensong at Westminster Abbey, where he heard the
following text:*

Not by might,
nor by power,
but by my spirit
saith the Lord of Hosts.

Zechariah 4:6

*Inspired by these words, he returned determined to proceed with the
building of the first great cathedral in England since the Reformation.*

80

The poetry of history lies in the quasi-miraculous fact that once on this earth, once on this familiar spot of ground, walked other men and women as actual as we are today, thinking their own thoughts, swayed by their own passions, but now all gone, one generation vanishing after another, gone as utterly as we ourselves shall shortly be gone. This is the most familiar and certain fact of life, but it is also the most poetical, and the knowledge of it has never ceased to entrance me, and to throw a halo of poetry round the dustiest record that Dryasdust can bring to light.

G. M. TREVELYAN:
Recreation of an Historian

81

At the end of the day:

For though the day be never so long
At last the bells ringeth to evensong.

STEPHEN HAWES: *The Passetyme of Pleasure*

82

History
Is the continuing story of man
It is here and now,
Yesterday,
To-day and tomorrow,
It is an ever-flowing stream.

The Resurrection of Christ
Is both an historical and an eternal fact.
It was real to those who lived in the past
It is real for us who live in this present time
It will be real for those who live in time to come.

H. M. Ll.

83

If I should die and leave you here awhile,
Be not like others sore undone, who keep
Long vigils by the silent dust and weep.
For my sake turn to life again and smile,
Nerving thy heart and trembling hand to do
Something to comfort weaker hearts than thine.
Complete these dear unfinished tasks of mine,
And I, perchance, may therein comfort you.

H. PRICE HUGHES

. . . after a storm there follows a great calm

84

When shall I enjoy a solid
peace, a peace never to be
disturbed and always secure,
a peace both within and
without, a peace every way
assured?

As long as we carry about this
frail body, we cannot be
without sin, we have lost also
true blessedness.

We must, therefore, maintain
patience, and wait for the
mercy of God, until iniquity
pass away: and this mortality
be swallowed up of life ...
Peace shall come in the day
which is known unto the

Lord; and it will not be day or night, such as it is at the present,
but everlasting light, infinite brightness, steadfast peace and
secure rest, because after Winter comes Summer—after night
the day returns, after a storm there follows a great calm.

THOMAS À KEMPIS

85

Peace I leave with you, my peace I give unto you: not as the world giveth, give I unto you. Let not your heart be troubled, neither let it be afraid.

John 15:27

86

In every moment of time you live where two worlds cross,
In every moment of time you live at a point of intersection.
However, living in time, you must live also now in Eternity.

T. S. ELIOT: The Rock

87

Do not stand at my grave and weep
I am not there. I do not sleep.
I am a thousand winds that blow
I am the diamond glints on snow.
I am the sunlight on ripened grain
I am the gentle autumn rain.
When you awaken in the morning's hush,
I am the swift uplifting rush
Of quiet birds in circled flight.
I am the soft stars that shine at night.
Do not stand at my grave and cry,
I am not there; I did not die.

Anon., found in the papers of Stephen Cummins,
a British soldier killed in Northern Ireland

In every moment of time you live
at a point of intersection

ANNOTATED INDEX OF SOURCES

Anon. 5, 14, 15, 22, 68, 72, 76, 87

BARRY, Frank Russell (1890-1976). Anglican bishop and theologian. His distinguished career included periods as Archdeacon of Egypt and Vicar of St Mary's, Oxford. Bishop of Southwell from 1941 to 1963, he published some twenty books between 1922 and 1974. 58

Bible, the. 4, 12, 26, 60, 79, 85

BRACELAND, F. J. 38

BRONTË, Emily (1818-48). Novelist, one of the three celebrated Brontë sisters. The most romantic of the three, her best-known work is *Wuthering Heights.* 18

BUNYAN, John (1628-88). Author of *Pilgrim's Progress.* He learned his English from the Bible, fought on the Parliamentary side in the Civil War, and became established as a preacher. Imprisoned by the Royalists from 1660 to 1672, on his release he engaged in widespread evangelistic activity. His autobiography is entitled *Grace abounding to the Chief of Sinners.* 48

BUTTERFIELD, Sir Herbert (1900-72). Historian, master of Peterhouse College, Cambridge and Regius Professor. His *The Origins of Modern Science* (1949) inaugurated the world-wide development of history of science. 77

CARLYLE, Thomas (1795-1881). Scottish historian, essayist and moral teacher. Rector of Edinburgh University. An idealist, he hated creeds and churches, but believed that "the Religious Principle lies unseen in the hearts of all good men." 53

CLARK, Kenneth Mackenzie, Baron (1903-83). Art historian, director of the National Gallery, professor of Fine Art at Oxford and Chairman of the Independent Television Authority. Best known for his television series "Civilization" (1969). He was created a life peer in the same year. 3

Cloud of Unknowing, The. 45

CLOUGH, Arthur Hugh. 51

COLERIDGE, Mary Elizabeth (1861-1907). English poet, novelist and essayist, she began to write verse as a child. Her first novel was praised by R. L. Stevenson, and her last two collections of poems were published posthumously. 29

CYPRIAN, St (*c*. 200-58). Bishop of Carthage, played a major role in the development of the Western Church. His works include many letters and a famous treatise on the unity of the Church. Arrested under the first edict of Emperor Valerian and martyred in 258. 11

DANTE (1265-1321). Italian poet, author of the *Divina commedia*, which made him one of the few truly universal and timeless poets. His life was marked by his early love for Beatrice, who died young, and by involvement in political dissensions between the papacy and the empire. 64

DAWSON, Christopher (1889-1970). Catholic writer, scholar, cultural critic. Lecturer at Exeter University and theology professor at Harvard. Edited the *Dublin Review* from 1940. 75

DONNE, John (1572-1631). "Metaphysical" poet of both earthly and divine love. Born a Catholic, he took the Oath of Supremacy and progressed in the Anglican Church, becoming Dean of St Paul's. His two main collections of poems are the *Songs and Sonnets* and the *Divine Poems*. 49, 62

ELIOT, Thomas Stearns (1888-1965). Poet, playwright, critic and essayist, born in the United States. His best-known works include *Murder in the Cathedral*, *The Waste Land* and *Four Quartets*. 6, 20, 54, 73, 86

ELIZABETH I (1533-1603). The daughter of Henry VIII and Anne Boleyn, she succeeded to the throne of England after Mary Tudor, whom she had beheaded. She presided over a great literary and artistic flowering, the rooting of Anglicanism and the rout of the Spanish Armada. 44

Epitaph. 25

GEORGE VI (1895-1952). King of England from 1936, when he succeeded to the throne on the abdication of his brother, Edward VIII, and succeeded on his death by his daughter Elizabeth. His Christmas broadcasts during the Second World War, in which he struggled to overcome a painful stammer, especially endeared him to the nation. 8

GOLDSMITH, Oliver (1728-74). Poet, novelist and dramatist, born in Ireland. Unsuccesfully studied law in London , followed by medicine in Edinburgh. His reputation rests mainly on the novel *The Vicar of Wakefield*, the play *She stoops to conquer* and the volume of poems *The Deserted Village*. 31

HAMILTON, Robert B. 36

HASKINS, Minnie Louise (1875-1957). Author, educated in London, she supervised women's factory work during World War I, then lectured at the London School of Economics. Her best-known work, *The Gate of the Year*, was published in 1940. 1

HAWES, Stephen (?-1521). Poet, little known about his early life. Appointed Groom to the Chamber at the court of Henry VII in 1502. He dedicated his chief work, the allegory *The Passetyme of Pleasure* to the King. 81

HUGHES, Hugh Price (1847-1902). Methodist divine, pioneer of the "forward movement," he started and was first editor of the *Methodist Times*. He wrote several books, mainly on social and ethical Christianity. 83

Inscriptions. 17, 21

JULIAN OF NORWICH (*c.*1342-after 1413). English mystic and anchoress. On 5 May 1373 she received a series of revelations, or "showings," chiefly of the Passion and the Trinity, and twenty years later she wrote *The Revelations of Divine Love* as meditations on the original experience. 28, 57

KELLER, Helen (1880-1968). Born deaf, dumb and blind, she and her teacher, Anne Sullivan, revolutionized therapeutic techniques and probably did more than anyone else to prove that apparently insurmountable physical disabilites do not imply lack of mental ability. She learned to speak and became an author. 19

KENNEDY, John Fitzgerald (1917-63). Son of a former U.S. ambassador to Great Britain, he served in the navy in the Second World War. Elected thirty-fifth President of the United States in 1961, his promise was cut short by his assassination in November 1963. 2

KILMER, Alfred Joyce (1186-1918). American poet and critic. Published three volumes of verse, including the ever-popular "Trees," which appeared in 1913 in *Poetry, A Magazine of Verse*. 37

LEWIS, Clive Stables (1898-1963). Novelist and essayist, author of *The Screwtape Letters* and the ever-popular series of *Narnia* stories for children. The emotions behind his apparently tranquil life recently became the subject of a major fim, *Shadowlands*. 7

Ll., H. M.: the initials of Henry Lloyd—see page 1. 46, 50, 56, 82

LONGFELLOW, Henry Wadsworth (1807-82). U.S. poet, professor of Modern Languages and Literature at Harvard from 1836 to 1854. His best known works, *Ballads and Other Poems* and *Hiawatha*, date from this period, followed in 1863 by *Tales of a Wayside Inn*. 78

LYTE, H. F. (1793-1847). Anglican clergyman, poet and hymn writer. Scholar of Trinity College, Dublin. Best remembered for "Abide with me." 23

MASEFIELD, John (1878-1967). Poet, dramatist, novelist and journalist. Appointed Poet Laureate in 1930. Published over fifty books, beginning with *Salt Water Ballads* in 1902. 32, 43, 66

McCRAE, John (1872-1918). Canadian poet and doctor. Served as medical officer in the Boer War and World War I, which produced his best-known poem, "In Flanders Fields" and led to his death from pneumonia. 24

PATMORE, Coventry (1823-96). Poet, born in Essex and associated with the Pre-Raphaelite movement. His major work, *The Angel in the House*, deals with married love.He became a Catholic and then wrote mainly on mystical or religious themes. 61

Prayers. 9, 59

PRICE HUGHES, H. 83

Proverb. 30

RAUSCHENBUSCH, Walter (1861-1918). American clergyman and theology professor, he became the leading proponent of the Social Gospel movement with the publication of *Christianity and the Social Crisis* in 1907. 34

SARTRE, Jean Paul (1905-80). French philosopher, novelist and dramatist, best known as the leading proponent of Existentialism, and for personifying intellectual café life in Paris. His best-known work is *L'Etre et le néant (Being and Nothingness)*. He declined to accept the Nobel prize he was awarded in 1964. 13

ROSSETTI, Christina Georgina (1830-94). Poet, born in London, the daughter of Italian poet Gabriele Rossetti. A devout Anglican, influenced by the Oxford Movement, she wrote till near the end of her life, despite illness. Much influenced by the Pre-Raphaelite movement, which her brother helped to found. 40

SCHWEITZER, Albert (1875-1965). Born in Alsace, theologian, physician and organist. In 1913 he abandoned a brilliant academic career and became a medical missionary at Lambaréné in French Equatorial Africa (now Gabon). His methods aroused a good deal of controversy, as did his theological works. He was awarded the Nobel Peace prize in 1952. 10

STEVENSON, Robert Louis (1850-94). Scottish novelist, dramatist and poet. Best known for *Treasure Island* and *Travels with a Donkey*. 33

TAYLOR, Bayard (1825-78). American travel writer and poet, known as "the American Marco Polo." Wrote novels and more than a dozen volumes of poetry, but best remembered for his poem "Bedouin Song" and his translation of Goethe's *Faust*. 35

TENNYSON, Alfred, Lord (1809-92). Poet, born in Lincolnshire and educated at Cambridge. His *In Memoriam* (1850) remains his finest achievement. As Poet Laureate from the same year he wrote several plays and continued writing poetry till his death. Hugely popular, he was created a Baron in 1884. 41, 63, 65

TERESA OF AVILA, St (1515-82). Spanish Carmelite nun and mystic. Reformed the Carmelite Order in the face of strong opposition. Her autobiography is one of the classics of Spanish literature, and *The Interior Castle*, *The Way of Perfection* and other works remain enduring spiritual masterpieces. 16

TERESA, Mother (of Calcutta) (1910-). Born Agnes Gonxha Bojaxhiu in Skopje, then in Albania. Went to India in 1928, took vows in 1937 and moved to work alone in the slums of Calcutta in 1948. Her work, through her sisterhood the Missionaries of Charity, has spread around the world. She was awarded the Nobel Peace Prize in 1979. 55

THOMAS À KEMPIS (*c.* 1380-1471). Ascetical writer, most probably the author of *The Imitation of Christ*, perhaps the most influential work after the Bible in forming Christian spirituality. A Canon Regular, his life was devoted to writing, preaching and copying manuscripts. 84

THOMPSON, Francis (1859-1907). Catholic poet. Born in Lancashire, he studied unsuccesfully for the priesthood and then medicine. Saved from destitution in London by Wilfrid Meynell, he wrote several volumes of poems expressing a deep yet simple spirituality in the 1890s, including his best-known work, *The Hound of Heaven.* 69

TREVELYAN, George Macaulay (1876-1962). Historian, professor of Modern History at Cambridge. Best known as a pioneer social historian, his works include *History of England* (1926) and its companion *English Social History* (1944). 80

UNDERHILL, Evelyn (1875-1941). Writer on mysticism. Author of *Mysticism, The Mystic Way*, the later *Worship* (1936) and numerous other works, she also translated medieval mystical writings; in her later years she was a much-sought-after retreat director and became a keen pacifist. 42

VAUGHAN, Henry. 71

WESLEY, John (1703-91). Elder brother of Charles, the founder of Methodism. After teaching at Oxford and a spell as a missionary in the United States, he founded Methodist chapels and started the "United Society." A great open-air preacher, he had the gift of appealing directly to ordinary people, converting them to scriptural holiness of life. 27

WILCOX, Ella, née Wheeler (1850-1919). U.S. journalist, recognized as a poet for *Poems of Passion* (1883). Prolific writer of fiction and essays for periodicals. 47

WORDSWORTH, William (1770-1850). Romantic poet, above all of the Lake District, where he lived with his sister Dorothy. Author of several of the best-known poems in the English language. 39, 67

YEATS, William Butler (1865-1939). Irish poet, essayist and dramatist, born near Dublin. Helped to found the Abbey Theatre, for which he wrote several plays. Volumes of poems appeared from 1888 to *A Full Moon in March* in 1935. Associated with the Easter uprising of 1916 and a senator of the Irish Free State in the 1920s, he received the Nobel Prize for Literature in 1923. 74

Burns & Oates publish books of general Christian interest, including Lives of the saints, prayer, spirituality and mysticism, church history, doctrine and life, theology, philosophy, Bible reading. A free catalogue will be sent on request to:

BURNS & OATES, Dept A,
Wellwood, North Farm Road,
Tunbridge Wells, Kent TN2 3DR

Tel.: (01892) 510850 Fax: (01892) 515903